DOUBLE YOUR SALARY:
How to Influence
Compensation and Promotions

JOSEPH G. LECAK

ISBN: 1503003388
ISBN 13: 9781503003385
Library of Congress Control Number: 2014919238
CreateSpace Independent Publishing Platform
North Charleston, South Carolina

Disclaimer

The stories and examples in this book are used to help explain everyday issues and problems I have encountered on my journey of taking the mystery out of pay and promotions. They do not necessarily portray specific people or situations, and no real names have been used.

The book contains the opinions and ideas of the author, and is intended to provide guidance and information on the material addressed in the book. It is sold with the understanding that the author and publisher are not offering career or financial advice in this book. The reader should consult a professional career counselor or financial adviser before taking action on any ideas discussed in this book. The book is general in nature, whereas each reader's situation is by definition unique.

The author and publisher specifically disclaim all responsibility for any liability, loss, or risk, personal or otherwise, incurred as a consequence, directly or indirectly, of the use and application of any of the contents of this book.

Acknowledgments

In 2002, I was given the greatest gift a human being can receive: a second chance. I remember it as if it happened yesterday. I was given a thirty-six-hour window as to whether I would survive an undiagnosed liver ailment. On a Monday morning, I received last rites; I recall how peaceful I felt. During this process, I made several promises to myself if I survived, one of which is publishing this book.

I would like to thank the following people and organizations who have supported me personally and professionally over the years. If I missed anyone, I apologize. To the employees of McCormick and Company—most of the lessons I learned were forged during my fourteen years there, the greatest company in the world to work for. Special thanks to Steve Rafter, Keith Burnet, and the late Bob Poirier; each of you taught me to be a professional.

To the employees and owners of American Kiosk Management where I got to practice and experiment with all the lessons I learned from my time at McCormick and Company—what a ride. Special thanks to Max James and Linda Johansen-James. I want to acknowledge Andrew Lanzino, a young man with whom I developed a nine-year collaboration during my time at American Kiosk Management. Andrew allowed me to practice and sharpen my ideas on him, and he is the inspiration for this book. My hope is that Andrew carries forward all the work we did together, and gets a chance to mentor and make a difference in someone's life.

To my friends in Las Vegas, especially my Sunday golf buddies—thank you for making Las Vegas our adopted home. There is no place like Las Vegas.

I want to thank my family. To my brother Mike—I hope you will buy a copy. To my stepdaughter Gina and her husband, Phillip—their home was the birthplace of this book. My late stepfather, Henry Fetherolf—he, as tough as they come, encouraged me to take a shot. To my mother, Catherine Fetherolf—thanks for everything. I could not have written this book without the support of my wife, Rose, my partner and best friend.

A special thanks to my father, Patrolman Joseph G. Lecak, end of watch 10-26-1961. Please keep the families of fallen police officers in your thoughts and prayers.

Introduction

If you follow the news concerning the state of the American economy, the overwhelming theme is the steady decline of the middle class and the loss of well-paying jobs. According to the pundits, the American economy is creating nothing but low-paying jobs that do not provide a livable wage. This is a discussion best left to the economists, politicians, and statisticians who follow these trends for a living. What I am prepared to discuss is that employers in all professions are always looking for highly productive employees, and they are willing to pay a solid middle-class wage to obtain individuals who can increase the value of their businesses.

Thirty-six years ago, I entered the workforce as a young professional full of passion, energy, and a willingness to work hard. I had a romantic view of how business was conducted, and was convinced that if I worked hard, I would be rewarded with higher pay and promotions. During my first four years in the workforce, I wandered aimlessly across the country from job to job in search of the perfect employer. It was about this time that I realized the path I was following was never going to work, so I decided to take charge of my professional life. Looking back on this period in my life, I realize now that I was planting the seeds for this book. Once I realized that promotions and raises are a process, my salary doubled over the next six years and quickly doubled again as I entered my peak productivity years. I was earning a salary that allowed me to live an upper-middle-class lifestyle.

Fast forward to 2002. My wife and I were living a comfortable lifestyle when my world was turned upside down. I had a near-death experience in my midforties, and was suddenly confronted with my own mortality. When I recovered, I realized that there had to be more to life than the pursuit of job titles and money. It was at this time that my wife and I decided to relocate to Las Vegas. I accepted a position with a startup retail company that specialized in personal care products, and became part of a team that orchestrated explosive growth over the next four years. During those early years as the company rapidly expanded, we hired almost five hundred employees. The overwhelming majority of the people we hired were entry-level or young professionals just starting their careers.

I began to notice that the employees I had a close relationship with were making the same mistakes I made during my first few years of employment. They would get hired and quickly become disillusioned that they weren't receiving raises and promotions large enough or fast enough, and they would move on to the next job, hoping their prospects would improve. I realized that I could make a difference, and began sharing my early mistakes and successes with anyone who would listen. Within a short period of time, the employees I was working with began to see their pay increase, and on several occasions, they received promotions.

I came to the realization that raises and promotions were part of a process that could be actively managed by an employee. Employees who were willing to follow the path I had laid out found that they could dramatically increase their chances of receiving above-average raises along with increasing their prospects for promotion. In 2009, I began accumulating notes, anecdotes, observations, and personal experiences that form the basis of this book. If you follow the lessons presented, my experiences will show that you can increase your productivity and self-confidence, which are traits desired by all companies.

I do not share the views of the doomsayers who feel that the American economy can no longer produce good, solid, middle-class jobs that pay a livable wage. The jobs are out there for those who understand the process of preparing themselves to meet their employer's needs and expectations. Good fortune, everyone.

CONTENTS

CHAPTER 1
Do It Right the First Time

One of the guiding principles for any organization or individual is to strive for perfection. How many times have you heard or used the phrase, "That's good enough"? Think back to when you were doing a job or task, and your gut tells you that something is not right, but you proceed anyway. It happens all the time in both our personal and professional lives. Fixing a mistake can be embarrassing and time consuming, which makes it convenient to use the excuse it will be OK to let it slide this one time. Other excuses are, "I'll pretend I didn't see it," "It's so small they won't catch it," and "I'm too busy right now, I'll fix it later if it happens again." I can remember catching errors or mistakes at the most inopportune time, such as right before lunch or right as I was getting ready to leave for the day. It seems to happen all the time and to every organization. This is because people are human and they make mistakes. There are whole industries centered on finding and correcting errors. Some of the more visible are accounting audit firms, quality control departments, customer service departments, and outside consulting firms of all disciplines.

One of the excuses used is that no one or nothing is perfect. That statement by itself certainly sounds right on the surface. However, I would like to take a closer look at the business definition of perfect, and the hidden costs of not striving for perfection.

What if you are contracting for a service and the person you're looking to work with states, "I have a 98 percent success rate." Using percentages to describe performance can be very misleading and possibly catastrophic for your business. One of the problems with using percentages to measure performance is loss of perspective. On the surface, 98 percent sounds great and could possibly lead you into a business relationship with this company. If you look deeper into a 98 percent success rate, it might sound like this:

- If an airline stated, "We safely land ninety-eight out of every hundred flights," would you fly with that airline?

- If a heart surgeon said, "I have had only two out of every hundred patients die," would you let that person operate on you?

You see the point: perfection is not only attainable, but it should also be a goal.

Years ago, I worked in a glass factory that sold empty glass jars to a baby food company. As part of doing business, we had to have 100 percent compliance with every jar sold; anything less had to be destroyed or we risked losing a very lucrative contract. We put in redundant quality inspection stations; we had very specific quality criteria at key points along the assembly line to ensure 100 percent of the bottles met standards. Did we produce perfect jars from the outset? No, but by the time the bottles entered the market, they were free of defects.

The major concern from the baby food company's perspective is that a jar with a defect, such as a bird's swing (a strand of glass sitting in the opening), would get filled, and the baby would later ingest shards of glass. One mistake would have ruined both companies. Imagine a worker who is tired, angry, or distracted letting a defective baby jar pass inspection, and the consequences associated with this single moment.

I would like to spotlight several examples that have been front and center in the news that highlight where an organization did not do it right the first time.

General Motors' recall of millions of automobiles with a defect in a small part was allegedly known early on, but was not acted upon when first discovered. The results have been death, reputations ruined, and billions of dollars' worth of rework. Some of the most famous business disasters were probably preventable if the do-it-right-the-first-time mentality had been applied: for example, Chernobyl, Three Mile Island, the BP oil spill, the *Exxon Valdez* crash, and the Space Shuttle *Columbia*.

In our daily lives, simple tasks such as paying bills, checking payroll, looking over an e-mail before hitting Submit, and turning in an accounting spreadsheet are all examples of doing it right the first time. Having to redo any of these simple daily tasks can have disastrous consequences to reputations (yours and the company you work for); they can be embarrassing, or worse, cost you your job. Think about the times you have been distracted, angry, tired, and hungry, or it's late in the day and you want to go home. You know better, but you still hit Send, Submit, or Send for Payment. You convince yourself that it will be fine this one time because you have never had a problem before. You must fight the urge to bypass the policies and procedures set up to avoid the type of errors that come with the thought it will be OK this one time because it always has been in the past.

Let's examine a function that every company is faced with on a daily basis: the payment of bills from vendors for services and goods. Your job as the accounts payable clerk is to make sure that all bills are paid accurately and on time.

Company procedure dictates that prior to paying invoices, you must match the packing list with the invoice to ensure that there are no over- or underpayments. One vendor in particular, Company XYZ, supplies a critical component for the widgets your company produces. Over the years, you have noticed that Company XYZ's invoices are always correct and are easy to process for payment, requiring very little review on your part. One day, you get a bill from Company XYZ; it's late in the day on the last day of an accounting month, and you have a deadline to process all bills received that day. You look the bill over and say to yourself, "The bills are always right. I'll just pay it this one time without reviewing the packing slip for accuracy." Months later an external audit discloses an overpayment of $10,000 due to a keypunch error made when an employee of Company XYZ entered the wrong amount shipped. Your company's procedures dictate that before any bill can be submitted for payment, the quantity on the packing list must be matched with the quantity on the invoice. The packing list correctly identified the error, but you did not check it against the invoice, which results in a $10,000 overpayment, a disciplinary write-up, and your boss's loss of confidence in you.

There are several lessons to be learned from this chapter that will serve you well throughout your career:

1. Think in terms of absolutes and not percentages, such as units, number of occurrences, and dollars.

This will keep you focused on the concept that all it takes is one incident to wipe out years of profits, cost you your job, or your boss loss of confidence in you.

2. Fight the urge to short circuit tried-and-true policies and procedures that are specifically designed to prevent the types of errors most commonly committed.

3. It can be very expensive to not do it right the first time.

CHAPTER 2
Rule of 72

Understanding the Rule of 72 is the most important lesson I have learned about the value of money and how it grows. The Rule of 72 is an easy mathematical equation that takes the mystery out of money and what it can do for you. The Rule of 72 is a simple formula to determine how quickly money will double in value over time. Money grows in value over time through the power of compounding interest. You might be wondering what this has to do with career planning; my answer would be quite simply: everything.

Let's start with an entry-level salary of $30,000 or $15 an hour for a full-time position. When can I expect to double this salary to $60,000 annually? At this level of salary, you are now entering what I would consider the middle class, with the next major step being an annual salary of $100,000, which in my opinion puts you squarely in the upper middle class. The Rule of 72 can take the mystery out of ascending the salary ladder and help guide you as to when to change jobs or ask for raises, as well as help you understand the annual performance review that dictates the raises you receive.

The Rule of 72 is a very simple math equation that tells you, based on your annual raises, when you can expect to double your entry-level salary. If you take your annual raise percentage and divide that into seventy-two, you get the answer as to how many years it will take to double your current salary. At an annual raise of 3 percent, which is standard in today's economy, you would divide seventy-two by three and get twenty-four years. A twenty-five-year-old making $30,000 annually who receives a standard raise of 3 percent will be earning $60,000 at the age of forty-nine. I don't know about you, but this does not sound appealing.

At an annual raise of 6 percent, which probably rewards highly productive work over a long time, you would divide seventy-two by six and get twelve years. A twenty-five-year-old making $30,000 at 6 percent annual raises will be earning $60,000 at the age of thirty-seven. This sounds much better, and you can begin to see the power of compounding money.

Rule of 72 Salary Chart
Years It Takes to Double a Starting Salary of $30,000

Annual Raise	Age	Equation	Years to Double Salary	Ending Age
3%	25	72/3	24 Years	49
4%	25	72/4	18 years	43
5%	25	72/5	14.4 years	39
6%	25	72/6	12 years	37
7%	25	72/7	10.3 years	35
8%	25	72/8	9 years	34
9%	25	72/9	8 years	33
10%	25	72/10	7.2 years	32
11%	25	72/11	6.5 years	32
12%	25	72/12	6 years	31

Now that you have the concept of the Rule of 72, you can see how it could help keep you focused and properly planning how you want your salary to work for you. In a real-life environment, huge annual raises year in and year out are probably not the norm. Most companies have a set structure designed to keep 70 percent of their workforce on a standard raise usually tied to inflation. The bottom 10 percent of the workforce may get nothing or be fired, and the top 20 percent may get the standard raise plus a one-time bonus that does not allow for the power of compounding.

Over my almost forty years of professional life, I have seen the following scenarios play out consistently from company to company that allow for maximum salary growth.

1. There are two times when working for an employer that you have a real opportunity to influence your earning power. The first time is when you are hired and have a realistic chance to negotiate your compensation and job title. The second time, ironically, is when you leave your current job to accept employment with another company, where you negotiated a great deal for yourself.

If you're an employee in good standing, there is the possibility that your current employer will make a counteroffer that will allow you a chance to negotiate a better deal for yourself.

2. Normal raises are just that—an attempt by the company to give the illusion of rewarding performance. In reality, only a few standout employees are well compensated; the rest get inflation-adjusted raises. By understanding the process companies go through when issuing raises, you can begin to formulate a plan to maximize your long-term earning potential. The annual performance review is a long drawn-out event designed to determine if an employee is worth keeping on the payroll. The actual

raise process is usually predetermined, and is nothing more than a few keyboard strokes sent over to an outside payroll company to administer.

3. Employees tend to take the raise process personally and subsequently lose motivation. How many times have you seen examples where an employee will lose motivation right after a performance review and starts posturing to leave or just flat-out quits? This is the worst mistake an individual can make.

Let's examine each point in no particular order, starting with point 3. If you quit a job because your raise did not meet your expectations, you are most likely giving away massive future earning potential. I have never seen an employee who abruptly quits over the issue of a raise make a sound decision. Most likely the employee is taking a similar job, for the same pay, and in all likelihood delaying future raises another year.

An employee in good standing should never take the raise process personally. If we examine point 2 from the company's perspective, the annual raise process is not meant to insult or keep you from the raise you deserve. Quite simply, your job is worth a certain pay level to the company. For the most part, raises are predetermined based on budgets, and are designed strictly to give the illusion of pay for performance. Determining raises is an integral part of the company's profit-and-loss statement, especially because payroll in most companies represents the largest single cost of doing business. Raises are designed to keep costs in line with revenue, not necessarily to reward performance.

This leads us to point 1 and an employee who is making $30,000 annually. This employee understands the Rule of 72 and is faced with the decision of accepting a position with another company. We will take a look at several scenarios for a twenty-five-year-old who starts at a salary of $30,000 and wants to double that salary in six years. I will demonstrate several strategies, both successful and failed, to help guide you through the power of the Rule of 72.

Our stated goal at the beginning of the chapter was to be earning $60,000 by the age of thirty-one. With proper planning, patience, and understanding, anyone with a marketable set of professional skills, education, and willingness to work hard should be able to execute this strategy.

I would like to start with a classic example of a failed strategy for maximizing earning potential that I have seen play out over and over again. Employee A is twenty-five years old and is starting out at an annual salary of $30,000. After the first year, this employee gets an annual raise of 3 percent and is now earning $30,900. In the second year, there is another 3 percent annual raise, and so Employee A is now earning $31,827. We are at the point in the story where our employee starts to make the classic mistakes that will completely sabotage future earning power. After the annual review, Employee A is unhappy with the amount of the raise being offered; to make matters worse, Employee B, who does the same type of work, received a promotion with more money.

Employee A hastily starts a job search and accepts a position with Company X for $32,000. The job starts in August, a key month because Company X's annual raises take place at the start of the new year. Let's move forward four months. Company X informs Employee A that employees must be with the company six months before being eligible for raises; therefore, Employee A will not be eligible for a raise until the beginning of year four. Moving forward to year four, Employee A receives a standard raise of 3 percent and is now earning $32,960. Year five comes around, and again Employee A receives a 3 percent raise, bringing total annual compensation to $33,949.

The Wrong Approach for a Twenty-Five-Year-Old with a Starting Salary of $30,000

Year	Raise Percentage	Dollar Amount	Ending Salary
Year 1	3%	$900	$30,900
Year 2	3%	$927	$31,827
Year 3	Changed Jobs	N/A	$32,000
Year 3	No Raise	$0	$32,000
Year 4	3%	$960	$32,960
Year 5	3%	$989	$33,949

Let's recap all of the mistakes Employee A has made over the last five years.

1. Leaving the previous company in year two due to dissatisfaction that another employee received a promotion and a better raise. Employee A would have been better off staying with the old job and accepting the series of 3 percent annual raises. If Employee A had stayed, at the end of five years the employee's annual pay would have been $34,778. Making an emotional decision to leave in year two cost this employee $839 in annual salary along with the power of compounding.

2. Mistake number two was leaving a job without coming away with a promotion and a significantly higher raise. If you recall, we noted two times when pay can significantly increase: when you accept a new position and when you leave an old position.

Let's examine what would have happened if Employee A had followed the plan laid out earlier in this chapter. Assuming the first two years would have been identical to our previous example, after year two our employee would be making $31,827. After the year two performance review, Employee A decides that a change in jobs is required, and calmly starts a job search. A rule of thumb I use is never to leave a job for another one unless there is a 20 percent increase in salary. With that knowledge, Employee A targets jobs that pay $38,500. An offer comes in from Company Z in August, which is accepted. In our previous example, Employee A did not cover the timing of the next raise and gave away a year of earning power. This time, Employee A negotiates to be eligible for a raise during the next review cycle. Company Z agrees. Four months later, Employee A receives a 3 percent raise, bringing compensation to $39,655. Years four and five bring 3 percent annual raises; thus, the compensation at the end of year five is $42,070. By following the simple rules laid out in this chapter, annual compensation is $8,121 higher when compared to an employee who acts upon emotion and does not allow the power of compounding work to increase earning power. By the way, the increase is over the life of this employee and not just a one-time yearly increase. This is a great start, but still does not give us the doubling of salary in six years that employees are capable of.

A Better Approach for a Twenty-Five-Year-Old with a Starting Salary of $30,000

Year	Raise Percentage	Dollar Amount	Ending Salary
Year 1	3%	$900	$30,900
Year 2	3%	$927	$31,827
Year 3	Changed Jobs 20%	$6,673	$38,500
Year 3	3%	$1,155	$39,655
Year 4	3%	$1,190	$40,845
Year 5	3%	$1,225	$42,070

Additional steps need to be followed to achieve a salary of $60,000 at the end of year six. The process I have observed countless times for someone who is twenty-five years old is that he or she should be able to double the entry-level salary in six years or less. The same process outlined should also work for the next double to $120,000, which should happen somewhere in the late thirties to the very early forties. The second double from $60,000 to $120,000 is difficult but achievable. A subsequent doubling to $240,000 is rare, especially as an employee collecting a paycheck.

Let's discuss how to position you for that salary of $60,000. We will discuss specific behaviors in subsequent chapters, but for now, I want to concentrate on what typically happens to an employee with skills and aptitude working for an employer who appreciates and rewards talent.

Employee A enters the workforce at age twenty-five at an annual salary of $30,000. As previously outlined, in the first two years, standard raises of 3 percent are received and result in an annual salary of $31,827. Sometime between years two and three, Employee A receives a promotion or takes a better position with another company. Employee A negotiates a 20 percent raise and no loss in the continuity of raises, which results in an annual salary of $39,655. The employee gains more confidence during years four and five, and negotiates raises of 6 percent if certain measurable performance objectives are met. (We will cover how to do this in later chapters.) At the end of year four, our employee performs admirably and receives a 6 percent raise, bringing compensation to $42,034. In year five, our employee receives a raise of 5 percent, bringing compensation to $44,036. It is year five and we are still $15,000 from our goal of $60,000 by the end of year six.

Our employee is now a seasoned professional, a self-starter with numerous traits coveted by corporate America. The employee is just entering a peak period of productivity and earnings power. If all goes according to plan, our employee has fifteen highly productive years left. From my experience, this employee has maximum value to corporations, which will pay for highly productive employees. Armed with confidence and self-awareness, Employee A plans to take advantage of that experience and knowledge and test the job market. Not surprisingly, multiple offers are presented, including one from the current employer. Employee A negotiates a 30 percent raise to $58,500 along with no loss in the continuity of raises. At the end of year six, our employee receives a 3 percent raise, bringing year six annual compensation to $60,225, thus meeting the six-year goal of doubling the entry-level salary of $30,000.

Targeted Approach for a Twenty-Five-Year-Old
with a Starting Salary of $30,000

Year	Raise Percentage	Dollar Amount	Ending Salary
Year 1	3%	$900	$30,900
Year 2	3%	$927	$31,827
Year 3	Changed Jobs 20%	$6,673	$38,500
Year 3	3%	$1,155	$39,655
Year 4	6%	$2,379	$42,034
Year 5	5%	$2,002	$4,036
Year 6	Changed Jobs 30%	$14,464	$58,500
Year 6	3%	$1,725	$60,225

CHAPTER 3
Negotiating Deadlines and Goals

An important but seldom used skill is negotiating deadlines and goals. How many times can you think of when your boss comes in, drops a pile of work on your desk, and states he needs this by the end of the day? In the meantime, you are working on a previous project that is also due at the end of the day. Frustration and anger set in. You quietly seethe and do your best to finish both projects. You complete the tasks on time, but neither is done to your standards, and most likely they contain shortcuts, or worse, errors.

The same scenario plays out with the setting and meeting of goals. Your boss sets a performance goal that you had no input in, and to make things worse, your compensation is contingent upon reaching goals you had no say in choosing. This ties in perfectly to our previous chapter of doing things right the first time. Employees have a much better chance of success if they have a direct say in negotiating the tasks and goals that they will be held accountable for, especially when compensation is involved.

When working on a project, always remember that deadlines are negotiable. Let's look at the example presented above. You're working on a project that must be done at the end of the day. You have properly planned out your day, and you are comfortable that you can complete this task when due. After lunch, your boss brings a new stack of work and also wants it done by the end of the day. You quietly agree, knowing you have no chance of finishing either task unless you take shortcuts.

The other option that is always available is to negotiate your workload with your boss so that everyone is satisfied. The key is to find out which task is most important and which can be renegotiated. In all likelihood, after professionally discussing the projects, both of you will agree on new deadlines. If the boss states both are critical and need to be finished at the same time, ask for help—it is not a sign of weakness. Remember that deadlines are always negotiable with proper notice and a professional presentation made to the person who agreed upon the original deadline.

There are several dos and don'ts when renegotiating a new deadline.

1. Don't wait until the last minute to ask for an extension.

2. Don't ask for an extension after the original deadline has passed.

3. Don't agree to unreasonable deadlines that put the accuracy of the work at risk. Remember, it is more expensive to correct errors. Do it right the first time.

4. Don't be afraid to ask for help or an extension.

5. Do give the person who agreed on the deadline reasonable notice that you will not make the deadline. It is at this point you are giving the person on the receiving end of the work the option to renegotiate a new deadline or shift resources if the original deadline is critical.

6. Do get the renegotiated deadline date in writing (e-mail) if possible.

7. Do self-check your work before turning it in. Remember: do it right the first time.

Negotiating goals works the same way as negotiating deadlines, except that the time horizon is usually longer. One major difference for me between deadlines and goals is I like to tie meeting goals to my compensation. Goals can be defined as short term, midrange, and long term. All short- and midrange goals should support the long-term goals of your company. It is imperative if you want to maximize compensation that all of the goals you are working toward go hand in hand with how the company generates revenue. I use short- and midrange goals as road maps to reaching my long-term goals. The worst thing that can happen during the annual compensation review is a surprise at the end of the year that a goal won't be met. This is not the way to earn a promotion and more compensation.

Short-Term Goals

I use short-term goals as mile markers on a highway that I want to reach on my way to my ultimate destination. If I find that I'm lagging, I have the option to go faster in order to maintain my pace. Typically, you won't panic and ask for a renegotiated goal at this point. This is the time to assess where you're at and determine what additional steps might be needed to get back on course. In baseball terms, seasons are long (162 games), and ups and downs occur routinely as part of the process. You don't bench your star player or trade him after fifteen games. You would look at indicators to determine what might be causing the player not to perform to expectations. You might look at the health of the player or maybe give the player a day off, but at this point in the season, you would not overreact.

Midrange Goals

As you approach the midrange of your long-term goal, this is the time to assess whether the original goal you agreed to is still attainable, or do you need to reset the goal with mutual agreement from your boss. You cannot just walk into your boss's office and announce, "I'm not going to make plan; I need to reduce the goal by half." The process of negotiating a goal should be painful, carefully laid out, with no excuses offered, just facts. Continuing with our baseball example, teams routinely use the all-star break (midseason) to evaluate their goal of making the playoffs. Well-managed baseball teams that realistically understand their chances of meeting their goals will add players (resources) or trade aging stars in preparation for next year. Well-run business organizations act the same way. They do not throw good money after bad in hopes of reaching an unattainable goal. As part of the process of renegotiating goals, expect some backlash. In baseball, the fans and media will voice their opinions. In business, you can expect much the same from your superiors.

Long-Term Goals

My philosophy on setting long-term goals is that they must be achievable while stretching the team. Using our baseball analogy, the long-term goal of every team should be to win the World Series; however, at the end of the season, only one team can achieve this goal. There are thirty professional baseball teams, and twenty-nine teams will ultimately fail. As part of the process of winning the World Series, ten teams make the playoffs to get a chance to participate in the World Series. As part of setting long-term goals while stretching the team, I would submit that the long-term goal of each of the thirty teams should be to make the playoffs. Once a team determines that it will reach the playoffs, it can then set about the process of renegotiating its long-term goal to possibly include winning the World Series. It works the same way with your personal life and professional life. Set an attainable goal that stretches yourself and the team. If you discover during the process that you will reach that long-term goal, you can then go about the process of stretching further for a higher goal.

Monitor your long-term goals using short- and midrange goals and course correct as needed. Think of your short- and midrange goals like you do your car dashboard. You don't need to look at your gas gauge constantly, but you do need to occasionally glance at it to determine if you will meet your long-term goal of reaching your destination without running out of fuel. Once you determine whether you can meet your long-term goals, you can readjust both up and down.

Continuing with our baseball analogy, there comes a point in the season when a team realizes that just making the playoffs is too light a goal; therefore, they begin to readjust their original long-term goal of making the playoffs to now include reaching the World Series. The exact opposite is true when a team realizes that the goal of making the playoffs is unattainable; the team now sets a lower goal of planning for the next season.

CHAPTER 4
The Art of Language and Words

There may be nothing more important to your career than what you say and how you say it. This can be the difference between moving forward in an organization and being left to ponder why you are stuck in a dead-end job. If you find yourself wondering why Sally got promoted and you didn't, or why Bill got the corner office while you're still in a cubicle, or how come John can afford a new car and your car is ten years old, the answer may be the proper use of language and words in a professional work environment. Use of proper words and language requires practice and habit. Let's examine common words and phrases and their hidden meanings.

1. Try—When I hear the word *try*, my interpretation is you are giving yourself permission to fail. The

Merriam-Webster online dictionary definition of *try* is to make an effort to do something: to attempt to accomplish or complete something. Nowhere does the word *try* imply that a person *will* accomplish or complete something. How often have you heard, "At least I tried"? Granted, this is laudable, but I want people who use words like *will*, *must*, *determined*, and *can do* over people who "try." When you are expressing your willingness to take on new tasks, avoid the word *try*, which implies it's OK if you don't complete your task because at least you tried.

2. "I'll do better next time"—This phrase implies that there will be a next time. My response to employees who use this phrase is, "How come you didn't do better this time? What will be different the next time?" There is an old saying that you only get one time to make a good first impression. Give your best every time. You'll never regret it, and you won't have to apologize for not performing better.

3. "I need more"—When you use this phrase without offering specifics about what you need, you open yourself up to someone else's interpretation of what it is you're asking for. Working in retail, I was on the receiving end of "I need more" requests with no explanation of exactly what was needed. When I reached out to find out what was needed, more often than not the person making the request could not articulate the need, and so would end up getting

nothing. When you ask for additional resources, it is imperative that your requests are specific to the task, are logical, and within a company's budget. Employees who articulate their needs will always take precedence over employees who cannot offer specifics as to why they need more. If you consistently get what you ask for, you will get more opportunities to successfully complete your tasks and goals, which leads to the opportunity to earn more money.

4. "Around"—The use of this word implies to come near, close to the actual, but not completely accurate or exact. Everything about this word is the opposite of how you should be communicating. When I hear "around," I'm hearing you're not capable of meeting the requirements.

5. "No one told me"—This phrase usually means you neglected to do something. If you miss a meeting, a deadline, or didn't follow company procedures, imagine how it sounds when you respond, "No one told me." If you have to be told every minute detail about how you are expected to perform or behave, you will not thrive in a professional environment.

6. "I wasn't trained"—Be very careful when you use this phrase; I'm not sure it should ever be used even if it is warranted. The only reason for the caution is that there are better ways to communicate a lack of training to your employer. My expectations for

someone I hire are that certain types of skills and behaviors—such as housekeeping, workplace behavior, math, spelling, and other life skills—should come with you and are not my responsibility to train. Let's examine a common problem of employees not cleaning up after themselves in the lunchroom. This is not caused by a lack of training, but by sheer laziness. Housekeeping is nothing more than putting the effort to keep your area neat and clean and does not require training. At the other end of the spectrum is an employee being thrust into a job assignment where training would be required using proprietary computer programs or an in-depth knowledge of a complex product that needs to be communicated to customers before a sale occurs. As an employee, once you are presented with a task that you are not trained for, it is up to you to ask for the training you need before moving forward. It can be disastrous to embark on a task without alerting anyone that you are not properly trained. If you feel you don't have the necessary training, the time to say so is before you start, not after you create a mess and blurt out, "But I wasn't trained."

7. "I'm too busy"—This is my absolute favorite. Over my thirty-five years, I have heard countless employees utter this phrase. Early in my career, I had an employee who said this all the time to avoid work. As an inexperienced manager, it can be very

difficult to confront someone who gives the illusion of being busy. To prove a point to myself, I decided that I was going to take away all the job functions this employee had and either do them myself or give them to more productive employees. When I had done this, the employee was left with nothing more than part-time work. I measured the output and time it took to complete the remaining tasks, and determined that about twenty hours of work was being done even though I let the employee work the full forty hours. Once I was confident that I had enough data to support my theory, I gave the employee a routine task that would take a couple of hours to complete. This employee immediately claimed to be too busy to take on additional work. I came to the conclusion that even if I took away tools such as phones and computers, and redistributed the tasks they were responsible for to other team members, employees who say "I'm too busy" would still complain about being busy. For the rest of my career, anyone who used that phrase without substantiating that claim I made sure would not be employed under my supervision. As an employee you are not too busy; you just have deadlines and goals that need to be met. One of my favorite sayings is, "If you want to get something done, give it to the busiest person in the room—they find a way."

Use of proper language in a business environment is nothing more than practice and habit. When communicating professionally, use words and phrases that are specific and measurable. Let's look at some examples.

Your boss brings in a task and asks when you can finish and present it. The wrong answer would be, "When I can get to it," "In a few days," or "Sometime next week." Notice these phrases leave it open to interpretation for several conclusions to be drawn by the person who needs the presentation. The first is that you don't know what it would take to get the job done. The second is that the person needing the presentation will just assign a deadline without your consent, or worse, make an assumption on when you will complete the task. These phrases also give you permission not to complete the task because you did not commit to a firm time and date. The correct response would be, "I can have it Friday by four o'clock." This gives your boss the opportunity to accept your deadline or renegotiate a new one. At this point, there is a very specific deadline that has been negotiated between employee and employer. The next step is up to the employee to meet that deadline.

Proper use of language works the same way when setting goals. You're in a meeting and the discussion centers on ways to increase sales. Because you are responsible for sales, you respond that sales should increase by 5 percent. On the surface, this sounds like a great goal— it's measurable and seems specific. A valuable lesson I learned over the years is to avoid the use of percentages when setting goals because they do not take into account that one single event can destroy a company.

An example of avoiding percentage-based goals is the glass-manufacturing company I used in the beginning of the book. The general manager stated that he wanted a 5 percent reduction in glass jar defects. What is not stated in this goal is that the 5 percent reduction still leaves 250 defects getting to the baby food filler, resulting in $1.5 million in returned goods. The 5 percent reduction goal sounds great and might even get accepted in less progressive companies. The more specific goal of eliminating 250 defects and $1.5 million in returned goods is the goal that should be presented and accepted. State your goals in measurable language such as units and dollars and avoid open-ended goals. The problem with vague, open-ended goals is that they leave room for catastrophic failures; imagine if an airline had a stated goal that it was acceptable for 1 percent of its flights not to land safely. The airline would immediately be out of business.

CHAPTER 5
Hard Work Never Killed Anyone

From my own experiences and speaking with hundreds of people, I've noticed that hard work has never killed anybody. In fact, I've noticed the opposite: when employees are fully engaged, have participated in the goals and objectives of the job, and understand why they are being asked to sacrifice, they become energized, highly motivated, and highly productive. To illustrate my point, let's look at some real-life examples.

Employee A is a young man in his late twenties with high aspirations. He wanted to move forward and was contemplating taking the CPA exam. He is married with one child and another on the way. Prior to embarking on the CPA exam, I had several conversations with him on how much work was entailed in passing the exam. After talking through that his job was secure, his family was supportive, and acknowledging the amount of time involved studying, I shared some of my experiences going for my MBA degree. I was working full time and studying forty hours a week. I never got sick, and when I had doubts about whether what I was trying to accomplish was worth the time and effort, I was able to refocus on achieving my goal. I was able to share with him that when I actually got my degree I was filled with a sense of accomplishment, and all the sacrifice and hard work quickly became a distant memory. I was lucky enough to observe this young man studying in his office after hours for almost two years, putting in countless study hours. When he finally passed all four parts of the exam, I asked him his thoughts on all the work he put in accomplishing his goal. He had almost the identical response that I had: the sense of accomplishment drowned out all the hard work.

Another recent example I observed was a young man I have been mentoring receiving his four-year college degree. It took him almost six years, including summer courses. This goal was accomplished while raising a family and working full time. When I asked him his thoughts on all the hard work, his reaction was identical to the others: the accomplishment overwhelms the memory of the hard work.

These observations help guide me whenever I waver on whether to begin an endeavor. Writing this book is a perfect example of the sense of accomplishment overwhelming the memory of the hard work. The concept for the book came to me five years ago, and after numerous revisions and adventures navigating the self-publishing process, my lasting memory will be of accomplishing my goal of publishing this book. The hard work and sacrifice fade away, while the satisfaction is forever.

The name of this chapter is "Hard Work Never Killed Anyone." This is true when hard work is tied to a sense of accomplishment where anything is possible. The opposite can be true also; hard work for hard work's sake can be demotivating and demoralizing.

We have all witnessed or been in situations where we were asked to do a task with no explanation, no input, and no opportunity to participate in the fruits of our labor. A valuable lesson I learned about hard work is that it has to be directly tied to results, and then it must be properly rewarded. Hard work for hard work's sake is pointless; imagine taking a pile of sand and shoveling it a few feet over to make a new pile of sand without the benefit of a plan or direction. If the same pile of sand was covering a water pipe that needed to be exposed for a leak, then this hard work has measurable results with a payoff.

One of the most destructive forms of behavior in a work environment is a boss wandering around making sure everyone looks busy. I can guarantee you it won't take long for employees to figure out the boss's behavior and then give the illusion of working hard. As an employee, you want a boss who understands the concept of hard work with results. As an exaggerated example, what type of employee is more valuable to an organization: Employee A, who manages to always look busy but never seems to produce measurable results, or Employee B, who creates millions of dollars of profit while managing to enjoy a day off every once in a while and doesn't always give the appearance of being busy? I'll take Employee B every time. If you want true earning power, align your interests with those who reward results, not hard work. I was lucky early in my career to work for a boss who told me, "I don't pay for hard work, only results." I use the example of what it must have been like to work on the pyramids. Imagine toiling long hours in the hot sun performing mind-numbing work, and spending a lifetime without ever seeing what your labor amounted to.

In order to be successful, it is extremely important that you put yourself in the proper setting to take complete advantage of your hard work. All successful companies cultivate this environment, and welcome individuals who display the type of characteristics that are outlined in this book.

CHAPTER 6
If You Don't Make It or Sell It, You Better Support It

In my early twenties after I had just received my degree in accounting, I jumped from job to job for several years and then landed a job with a plastics-manufacturing company as a staff accountant. At that time in my life a job was just a job, a way to pay rent and put food on the table. If you're reading this book, you probably know exactly what I'm talking about. I was an employee out on the fringe, performing routine tasks while the important work of manufacturing plastic containers was happening all around me. Basically I was counting what other people were being paid good money to do.

One day I went into my plant manager's office and asked what I needed to do to earn more money. He told me that if you don't sell it or make it, you better figure out how to support it. He then asked me the following question: "Are you willing to do whatever I need you to do?" In the same breath he said, "And oh, by the way, you're a salaried employee, so you won't be making any extra money." Since I had taken the initiative to go down this path, I did not hesitate. I said I was willing to do whatever he needed to be done.

The next thing I knew I'm working my regular staff accounting job Monday through Friday during the day and the midnight to eight o'clock shift on the weekends as a floor supervisor. The plant was experiencing a significant upturn in business, but the company did not want to make the investment to operate seven days a week until it was comfortable that the new business was stable. We operated seven days a week with a volunteer workforce on the weekends. When I was discussing this volunteer floor supervisor position, I asked the plant manager if I could go home on Monday morning to clean up and then return to work to my regular job. I was told to bring in a change of clothes and report to my desk as scheduled, which made for a sixteen-hour day. The weekends were never compensated because I was considered a salaried employee.

When I look back on this experience, it is clearly one of the most important steps I took in shaping my future compensation. As for the saying, "If you don't sell or make it, you better figure out how to support it," that took a few years for me to fully grasp what the plant manager was telling me. Understanding what this meant opened up the door for me to significantly increase my earning potential by making sure that I understood how the company I was working for generated its main source of revenue.

All companies have their primary source of revenue; study carefully the company you work for or are thinking of working for so you can become a productive and valued member of their team. As we discussed previously, be very specific when describing where the primary source of revenue comes from as this will help you focus on how your job fits in. Making stuff or selling stuff is not an answer (by the way, I have heard these answers from employees). A proper statement would be, "Company A sells teenage apparel online and in all the major malls in North America." To further describe Company A's primary revenue source, you would add the following to help you focus on where you should be concentrating your efforts: "Currently Company A derives 40 percent of its revenue online and 60 percent in its brick-and-mortar stores. Company A is forecasting this trend to reverse in two years, and the majority of its revenue will come from its online presence." A deep understanding of a company's primary focus can help you determine where the best opportunities are going to be to maximize your earning potential. I don't know about you, but if I were working for Company A, I would want to be involved with expanding their online business and creating value for my employer.

The reason it is important to determine how a company derives its revenue is that compensation usually flows to the people who create the most value. Work skills related to increasing sales and increasing unit production are easy to measure and compensate. You should be focusing your energy on getting into areas of the company that are highly compensated. If your passion and work skills can't be easily transferred to the sales and production areas of the company, remember the second part of the statement: "You better figure out how to support it." Some examples are the best way to illustrate this.

If you are in payroll, the best way to support selling and production is by correctly paying everyone on their scheduled pay dates. The easiest way to destroy morale in a company is to not pay employees on time or correctly. If you are in Human Resources you can support selling and production in a number of ways: solid employee benefits, consistent application of policies and procedures, compensation based on productivity, and solid hiring and promotion practices. If you're in Accounts Payable, you can make sure that all vendors are paid on time, ensuring that the company does not get put on credit hold, which can lead to increased borrowing costs and possibly disruption of raw materials needed for production. You can ensure that all payments are accurate and that the company pays only for the goods and services it receives.

CHAPTER 7
Delayed Gratification

In the previous chapter I was working in a plastics-manu-facturing company seven days a week: my regular job as a staff accountant during the week and a voluntary job as a floor supervisor on the weekends. During the week I was working from eight to five o'clock, and on the weekends midnight to eight o'clock. When the Sunday shift ended, I went straight to the front office and worked my account-ing job. The hours I worked on Saturday and Sunday were never compensated. My goal during all of this was to dis-tance myself from accounting and get involved where the company derived its revenue: the production and selling of plastic containers. I worked these hours on and off for the better part of a year whenever I was needed. Because business was good, I worked a significant number of sev-en-day workweeks. All during this time I never once dis-cussed pay with the plant manager. I wanted to make sure that first I had gained his confidence and that of the rest of the staff. My time for that discussion never arrived because the following year the plant manager left for a better opportunity with a much larger company.

I made the decision soon after to seek a better opportunity, and was able to demonstrate to prospective employers that I was willing and able to accept more responsibility and do whatever was needed in support of and participate directly with what the company made and sold. The important lesson here is if you want new opportunities, you need to make it easy for your employer to offer you opportunities. In my case I worked for free, so it was hard for my employer to pass on that. Once you receive the opportunity, it is imperative that you reach the goals you set for yourself. It was important to me that I be seen as a viable alternative for working directly on the manufacturing floor. I was determined to shed the label of just an accountant. I chose to delay gratification until I was confident that I had attained the skills that I thought the rest of the outside world would value. When I left the plastics company, I was handsomely rewarded by my new employer, and achieved my goal of doubling my entry-level salary in six years or less.

The important lesson to take away is that, early in your career, don't make earning more money your entire focus; the money will take care of itself if you concentrate on acquiring skills you can use for the rest of your life. Choose whom you work for wisely, make sure you understand exactly how the company earns its revenue, and work toward being able to perform in a number of different environments. Always remember your goals for compensation and move toward those goals once you are confident the skills you have acquired are transferable either with your current employer or a prospective employer. When you volunteer for a task, especially one that carries recognition and compensation, you must complete the task, be prepared to demonstrate the value you created, and at the appropriate time ask to be compensated for your work. There is a proper time and place to ask for more money. As we discussed previously, if annual raises are due soon, wait a few months as the conversation for more money is already on the table, and your request for additional compensation over and above a normal raise will be received better.

If you feel that the company won't fairly compensate you, it might be time to take your newly minted skills and see what the rest of the world has to offer. If you receive an offer from another company, don't be surprised if your current employer makes a counteroffer. This is a natural time to discuss additional compensation, and the conversation should flow smoothly.

We previously discussed that as an employee there are realistically only two times when large increases in compensation can be expected: when you first enter a company, and when you are leaving a company to pursue other opportunities. When you first enter a company you will never look better. You are excited to start your new job, you are full of passion and energy, and the company is excited to have you contribute to its success. When you plan to leave your current employer for another opportunity, if you are a valued employee, this represents the best of both worlds. You have the prospects of a new job and an exciting salary increase, and it is possible that your current employer values your work and is prepared to make an offer. This would be the sweet spot for salary negotiations.

It is important to remember when negotiating compensation that it isn't always about the money. Some companies are more bottom line-oriented about salary and have strict budget guidelines. Find out what is valuable to you and don't be afraid to ask. Remember, the time to ask is when you enter a new job and when you leave an old one. The list of non-money compensation you can ask for is endless and limited only by your imagination. Here are some of the more popular:

1. Additional time off with pay above and beyond the existing vacation policy.
2. A year-end bonus not tied to your annual compensation.
3. Company phone.
4. Company car.
5. Flexible work hours.
6. Help with your relocation expenses.
7. Help with your continuing education.

CHAPTER 8
Problem Solving

A general theme throughout this book centers on the ability to solve problems. Most of us have our jobs because of the problems that businesses encounter on a daily basis. Employees who can move beyond merely putting a Band-Aid on a problem and can permanently solve problems are in high demand and earn top dollar. Problem solving goes beyond the ability to merely identify problems and put in stopgap solutions; it's a skill that requires discipline and a well-defined process.

The goal of solving any problem should be to find a solution that prevents it from happening again. This statement has several dimensions I would like to explore.

1. As an employee, if you keep making the same mistake over and over again and cannot learn from your mistakes, you will not be employed for very long.

2. Implementing the wrong solution to a problem can be devastating to a company's reputation and bottom line.

3. Identifying the cause of a problem is the key to preventing it from reoccurring.

4. Once you determine the course of action you want to implement, it is critical that you measure your progress using short-, mid-, and long-term goals.

Over the years, I have witnessed numerous occasions where a company implements the wrong solution to a problem. This can be devastating to a company's reputation as well as to its bottom line. An example near and dear to most of us will help illustrate my point. Most of us have taken our cars in for service, and when asked by the repairman what the problem is, we either cannot tell him—we say the car just doesn't "feel right." We know something is wrong; we just can't say exactly what. The repairman tells you he will do the best he can and starts working on the car. Four hours later, you get an itemized bill for a new battery, new timing belts, a water pump, and a few other items you never heard of. The cost comes to $750. You pay the bill and drive off the lot. However, as soon as you hit highway speed, you feel the same problem. You take the car to another repair shop. Fifteen minutes later, the repairman comes out and tells you he tightened something in the engine block, charges you $50 for labor, and you drive off the lot with the problem solved. This is a perfect example of what can happen when the wrong solution is applied to a problem. In this case study, you spent four hours of your time and $750 to have the wrong solution worked on. Compare that to the fifteen minutes of your time and $50 when the right solution is applied.

Another example is when you schedule an appointment with a doctor because you don't feel well. The doctor asks what the symptoms are, and you say you ache everywhere. She prescribes some medicine, and after a few doses the side effect from the medicine is worse than how you originally felt. To make matters worse, your original symptoms are still there. You go to a specialist who now has to treat you for the side effects of the medicine and your original symptom of aching everywhere. After a couple of pointed questions from the specialist, you find out that your pain was caused by muscle cramps from not drinking enough water. Months later, you get a bill from the specialist for $1,500. If you had originally gone to the specialist, you would have had a bill for a $40 co-pay along with the cost of a few pennies for drinking more water.

Problems that occur in business work much the same way: if you implement a solution that has nothing to do with the original problem, you can create a much larger problem down the road that becomes more expensive to solve.

The examples of the car mechanic and the doctor highlight the importance of identifying the cause of a problem so you can implement the correct solution to keep it from reoccurring. Identifying the cause is the key to effective problem solving. Employees who can do this are worth their weight in gold. There are several steps that I have followed to determine if I have properly identified the cause of a problem.

1. I never problem solve in a meeting. Meetings should be brief, used to provide updates, and hold people accountable for fulfilling their goals. Meetings should also be used to set agendas and receive promises from colleagues on actions they are prepared to take.
2. I'm a big fan of Occam's razor (*Wikipedia*, s.v. "Occam's Razor," last modified November 10, 2014, http://en.wikipedia.org/wiki/Occam%27s_razor) which states that when you have several theories of the cause of a problem, the simplest one is best.
3. Test your ideas on a small scale so that if you still have not identified the cause, you will not have created more damage. A good example of this is when a doctor prescribes a topical medicine to be applied on the skin. You will be instructed to apply some on a small, inconspicuous patch of skin to see how the medicine reacts before liberally applying it everywhere.

4. Once you determine a course of action, measure the results. The final solution is always to prevent the problem from reoccurring. If the problem is complex, you may have to set a series of short-, mid-, and long-term goals to gauge how well the implementation of the solution is proceeding.

If you follow the steps outlined above, you will gain confidence in your ability to solve problems effectively. Once you gain a reputation as a problem solver, you should see rewards accrue to you in the form of prime work assignments, generous compensation, and promotions.

CHAPTER 9
Think for Your Boss

I have been lucky and also smart enough throughout my career to have had the opportunity to work with people who took an interest and mentored me. One of the most valuable lessons I received was to think for my boss. This was a hard lesson to learn and took time for me to fully understand. When you first look at this phrase "think for your boss," it sounds like either the boss can't think for himself or you are smarter than the boss. Nothing can be further from the truth. Once I fully grasped the subtlety of this statement, I realized it had several components.

Thinking for your boss means you should never present him or her with a problem without including a well-thought-out solution. What good does it do the organization if you state a problem and just dump it on the boss's desk for the boss to solve? At this point, you're really of no value to the organization. Problems without a solution are just griping. When you present a real problem, make sure you fully understand it and present a solution that is integral to the problem at hand. One of the worst possible outcomes to problem solving is committing resources to either the wrong problem or to a solution that doesn't work.

When presenting problems and solutions, get to the cause of the problem and identify possible solutions. Solutions should never be personal attacks; they should contain direct and measurable outcomes and, most important, solve the problem permanently. When I presented a solution to a problem, I always felt it was then up to the boss to determine where that solution fit into the bigger picture. If done properly, my problem identification and possible solution would stimulate further action and investigation.

When presenting solutions to a problem, determine what the cost of implementation entails. Don't guess if you don't know for certain, although it is acceptable to estimate a cost if your sources are good. In these situations, I preferred to overestimate and have the project come in lower. Your solution should include the number of personnel hours required, especially if interdepartmental resources are needed. I always discuss my ideas with my peers before committing other departments' resources. If you find that there are not enough internal personnel resources, investigate whether an outside company can do the job; this might even be cheaper in the long run.

As an example, imagine your solution requires labor to pack and ship a significant amount of product. It might be cheaper if you outsourced this project to a third-party company rather than burden your company's resources. When presenting a solution, it is critical that you understand exactly what your company does and how it derives its revenue. We covered this in Chapter "6", but it bears repeating. Let's take our example of packing and shipping a product a step further to drive home this point. If your company assembles widgets and then ships them throughout the country, would you present as a solution buying your own trucks, developing shipping software, and hiring drivers? The answer is simply NO. You would pick up the phone and call UPS.

The last step for problem identification and solution is to set a deadline for completion. Make sure the deadline is specific. If you cannot pinpoint an exact time or date, a well-researched estimate will suffice. Your estimate should fit in with the activities and goals of your company. A good example would be a retailer attempting to bring goods to market to take advantage of the Christmas season. To further our example, if I did not have a firm date, but I had confidence in providing an estimate, I would estimate that the deadline would be met early in the fourth quarter, so my boss would know that the solution could be implemented in time for the Christmas season without any extraordinary intervention or additional cost. Using the same example, if I receive different information and the estimation of completion is now late in the fourth quarter, this would tell my boss that without any additional activity, we might miss the Christmas selling season. The next step would then be to provide solutions so that the Christmas selling window can be exploited. Your solution should be specific, and might include the cost of overtime as well as the cost of shipping air freight rather than ocean freight. At this point, you have identified the problem and provided several solutions that included time and cost. It is then up to your management group to determine the next course of action.

Another example of thinking for your boss is e-mail communication. During my career, few things have been more annoying than asking for information and receiving an e-mail attachment with a spreadsheet full of numbers from which I have to draw my own conclusions. Whenever I receive something like this, I view it as a waste of my time and something I could have done for myself. On the surface, this might seem arrogant, but when you view this from your boss's perspective, it might sound something like this: "I should have just saved all the extra time and done it myself." To make matters worse, there is that inner voice in your boss's head that asks why I even have this person on the payroll. As an employee, you need to understand this dynamic. Suddenly, you have planted a seed of doubt about your ability to take direction, think on your own, and be given more responsibility. The worst-case scenario is that your supervisor may now think that you are expendable.

What should happen is the detail work that supports your conclusions should be summarized in the body of the e-mail in language that is time specific, addresses costs, and provides a deadline. You can't cover all questions your boss might have, but you have made that person's job much easier in terms of analyzing the data and helping to determine if additional information is required.

CHAPTER 10
Go with Your Gut

Numerous times during my career I was left with nothing but my gut feeling. I found this worked very well for me when, in ambiguous situations, there were several solutions to the problem. Here are several examples to illustrate this point.

I was investigating different ways to ship product around the country, and I came up with two options. The first was to stay the course and continue to introduce packages through UPS's ground system from the assembly point of the product. The second option was to utilize full trucks shipped to a predetermined location, and then offload the product and reintroduce the packages into the UPS ground system. At the time, option one was cheaper because we did not have enough volume to fill up a truck to take advantage of the economies of scale. I presented both options and recommended option two based on a gut feeling I had. By choosing option two, we gained operational efficiencies that saved us money, but because of our smaller volume, we were unable to lower our shipping costs. In other words, we would be increasing our overall costs to operate. To take advantage of the reduced shipping costs, we needed a specific volume, and our plan did not forecast those volumes for the next eighteen months.

My gut feeling was that we had always beaten our plan, and based on our current trajectory, we would reach the volume we needed in less than twelve months. I presented option two and recommended we absorb the extra cost and grow into the program. Senior management chose option two; we reached the needed volume in less than twelve months, with the additional benefit that we were able to continue growing without adding extra employees due to the operational efficiencies we had gained because we had chosen to proceed with implementation earlier than we had projected.

A gut feeling should never take the place of solid research and methods. What going with your gut can do is keep you from embarrassing errors that place you in a position to be second-guessed or worse. Throughout my career, I have relied on my gut feeling to avoid embarrassing situations. An example of this we have all faced is preparing spreadsheets that contain an enormous amount of data. Listening to your gut before turning the work in is great in situations like this. There were times when analyzing the cost of sales data I would expect to see a certain outcome based on historical data and trends. After finishing the work, occasionally I would get a completely unexpected result. Sometimes, the only filter you have before submitting your work is your gut telling you something isn't right, please listen. When this has happened to me, I employ a couple of techniques. If my deadline is still a few days away, I will put the work aside and take a fresh look in the morning. If that doesn't resolve my anxiety, I will ask for a fresh pair of eyes to look over the results. When you work with something so closely, sometimes you can't see the forest for the trees. If I'm up against a hard deadline, I will negotiate an extension, and if that is not possible, I will ask for additional resources. The work needs to be correct, not wrong and on time. When you take these steps, usually what you find is an easily preventable and correctable error, such as a wrong equation in an Excel spreadsheet, or a typo where you entered $100 instead of $10.

It is imperative that you learn how to review your own work for accuracy and turn in work you are proud of. An important tool in this process is to go with your gut feeling and act on it. Remember: it is not an error if you correct the work prior to submitting it as complete.

CHAPTER 11
The Cockroach Theory

As we progress through our careers and suffer through the lows and celebrate the highs, always keep in mind that the highs and lows can provide teachable moments. I tend to learn more from the lows I have encountered throughout my career. For this lesson, I want to concentrate on challenges that get discovered seemingly by accident.

Early in my career, I would stumble upon an issue that gave the appearance of being a one-time event. I would investigate the issue and either treat it as a one-time occurrence and ignore it, or try to correct it. I started noticing a pattern that the problem I had seemingly solved would not only manifest itself again, but also was actually worse than I had originally thought it to be.

After a few embarrassing trips to my boss's office to explain why I didn't stop these issues from reoccurring, I labeled these types of issues "the cockroach theory." The pest control industry warns you there is no such thing as a single cockroach; where there is one, there are more. Even though you don't immediately see them all, you know they are there; you just need to keep looking until you locate the source of the infestation.

As I gained more experience, I began to identify issues that fit the profile of "the cockroach theory." I can best illustrate this with a couple of interesting examples that happened to me. I was once responsible for two large warehouse buildings in New Jersey. One was located about two miles from the main production facility. We had just moved into this facility when I decided to pay a surprise visit to the second shift (four o'clock to midnight). I quietly entered the building around eight o'clock. To my shock, I noticed all the employees drinking while operating fork-lifts. I called a supervisor from the other building over to act as a witness because I knew I would be terminating the whole crew. As everyone was clearing out their lockers and waiting for cabs to take them home (several employees were in no shape to drive), one of the employees pleaded for his job, stating this was the first time he had ever done anything like this. I responded that of all the days and times I could have picked to visit, I happened to choose the only day that everyone decided to have a drinking party? Once I had time to think about what had just happened, I realized this event fell under "the cockroach theory." This was not the first time that this behavior had occurred; it was just the first time they were caught drinking on the job.

About five years ago, I received a call from a store manager letting me know that she had received a shipment meant for another store. On the surface this seemed like a one-time shipping error that did not require any follow-up. My experience taught me that there might be more to this story than just human error for this one shipment. I had my shipping supervisor look for something unusual that might explain this error. Sure enough, we located an error in the way the shipping instructions were loaded into the computer. All of the shipping locations were off by one line, which meant that every shipment for our weekly orders contained incorrect shipping addresses.

My hunch was correct, and this was a classic case of "the cockroach theory." If one shipment was wrong, they all could have been wrong, which proved to be the case when we investigated thoroughly. Luckily, we caught the error quickly and corrected all the ship-to addresses for the shipments that were still in the warehouse. We were also able to work with UPS to fix the shipments in their system that weren't delivered yet. We called all of the customers who received wrong product and worked out a return and replacement shipment schedule.

Having worked in retail for ten years, I used "the cockroach theory" countless times when confronted by what seemed to be issues that we would randomly encounter. We would come across issues such as missing deposits, product theft, missing inventory, cash deposits not made when scheduled, long periods of absence from the workstation, substandard housekeeping—the list was endless. Whenever we encountered these types of issues for the first time, we scrutinized them under "the cockroach theory" and kept looking to make sure there were not more occurrences.

A classic example of "the cockroach theory" happened to me when I was working in Brooklyn in the mid-1990s. At that time, one of my responsibilities included warehouse functions, with the warehouse manager reporting to me. He took a two-week vacation, and I decided to cover his responsibilities because I had been working at this facility for only two months. One day a truck showed up to be loaded, and a big ruckus ensued between the union forklift operators and the driver of the truck over whose responsibility it was to load the truck. Union regulations stated that the forklift operators were to drop the pallets on the dock, and it was the truck driver's responsibility to load the truck from there. I informed the driver of our rules and told him to start loading the truck. He refused, stating that was not the arrangement he had with our warehouse manager. I asked him what were the arrangements he had, and he proceeded to tell me he had paid $250 to have the truck loaded by my forklift operators.

I excused myself and asked the forklift operators what they knew about this. They confirmed the arrangement, and told me they would not load the truck without their cut of the $250. I called the owners of the trucking company, who confirmed the arrangement and told me that paying $250 to our warehouse manager had been standard practice for several years. I told the owners I was new to the Brooklyn facility and asked them to fax over copies of the checks made out to our warehouse manager for the last year. The fax machine ran for over an hour, and I eventually stopped it after I had copies of checks totaling over $5,000. This was the perfect scenario for "the cockroach theory": where there was one check, there were dozens. The warehouse manager lost his job. I severed relations with the trucking company involved, which cost them several hundred thousand dollars in revenue. The union forklift operators were put on notice.

As you gain more experience working through challenges and problems, you will find yourself questioning what seem to be random one-time events and trusting your instincts to look deeper to determine if the issues aren't more widespread. Sometimes, the only warning you get that something isn't right is a gut feeling or your inner voice telling you there is more to the story than what is on the surface: "the cockroach theory."

CHAPTER 12
20–70–10 Rule for Employees

The 20–70–10 differentiation rule is a human resource tool developed by Jack and Suzy Welch in their book, *Winning* (New York: Harper Business, 2005). The thought behind it is that in a large employee pool, 20 percent of your employees will be top performers, 70 percent will perform to expectations, and 10 percent will need to improve or find employment elsewhere. Once an employee leaves and a new one is hired, you reshuffle the deck so that you always improve from the bottom up. You would replace a low performer with a strong performer, and then someone from the previous 70 percent would fall into the 10 percent category. It's never quite that simple, but over time, the theory is sound and should lead to an ever-improving workforce.

I wanted to introduce the concept so that you can better understand the employee-evaluation process and use this knowledge to your advantage. Over the years in all the companies I have worked for, all employers ranked their employees to determine the top 20 percent, the middle 70 percent, and the lower 10 percent. In a well-run company, the lower 10 percent does not mean you were a poor performer; it just means that 90 percent of the employees performed better than you did. From these rankings, raises were determined, promotions given, and prime jobs assigned, usually to the top-20-percent performers. Being in the top 20 percent was an excellent sign that your job was safe, your pay and bonuses were generous, and you were in line for promotions when available. As we discussed in previous chapters, landing in the top 20 percent is the path to doubling your entry-level salary in six years or less.

What I'm attempting to do is give you the necessary tools to land in the top 20 percent. I worked for a company in which the top performers were identified and assigned to supervisors who had to make sure these top performers did not leave the company. If these top performers did leave, it was because the company was aware they were contemplating leaving and chose not to keep them. If one of these top performers left unexpectedly, the supervisor assigned received less of a bonus.

The vast majority of employees fall in the 70 percent range. Management is perfectly content with this group as long as the company is stable and there are no major shifts in the business model. Some of the signs that indicate you are in the 70 percent group is that you will receive reviews that state you are meeting expectations and that your performance is "acceptable," that is, steady but unspectacular. You will get a standard raise, usually indexed to inflation. When promotions become available, you will not be promoted even if there are no other internal candidates; the company will fill the position from the outside. This book can help the 70-percent group understand what it takes to be considered a top-20-percent performer.

For those employees who fall in the bottom 10 percent, well-run companies will be looking to replace you, period. The signs you are in the bottom 10 percent might look like this. You receive a series of escalating disciplinary notices under the guise of improving your performance. With a first notice, which might be nothing more than a verbal counseling session, chances for joining the 70-percent group are at their best. Once written disciplinary warnings begin, it is probably just a matter of time before you will be terminated. At review time, phrases such as "did not meet expectations," "improvement needed," or "unsatisfactory" are used to describe work performance. Don't confuse a review in which one specific skill warrants an "improvement needed" and you get a satisfactory overall grade. An employee in the bottom 10 percent will get unacceptable ratings across the board, and the overall performance level will reflect below average or worse. You most likely won't get a raise and will be given thirty or sixty days to improve performance.

CHAPTER 13
Align with a Mentor

An excellent way to speed up the learning curve is to align with a mentor. This can take many forms and include many different people. When you first start a new job, a mentor can be someone who walks around with you introducing you to all the people you will be working with, showing you where all the office amenities are, such as coffee, bathrooms, and lunchrooms. It can take the form of helping you with office etiquette, such as how to answer the phones correctly, when lunchtimes and break times are, not eating at your desk, etc. The most valuable mentors are what I would call a life coach. Lessons learned from this type of mentorship last a lifetime. From my experience, life coaches see the potential that you cannot see in yourself, and they work with you to obtain the skills necessary to reach that potential.

An example that has helped me understand the importance of coaching is how professional athletes reach their full potential. Those who achieve the highest level of performance all share one common trait: they readily accept coaching. Tom Brady of the New England Patriots is universally recognized as one of the top-five quarterbacks in history, and when he retires, he will be a first-ballot hall of famer. When he is inducted into the hall of fame, I guarantee he will acknowledge all his coaches, and there will be one or two who hold a special place with him. Everyone needs a coach.

When people take a genuine interest in your professional development, whether you sought their help or they initiated the contact, grab the opportunity and learn all you can. In Chapter "6", I discussed the time I sought advice on moving away from my accounting background and what I was advised to do to accomplish that goal. Looking back, the person who told me what I needed to do represented a mentor or life coach in my professional development. I followed that person's advice, and it was the start of a long and rewarding career path.

In addition to identifying a mentor, make sure that you identify friends and coworkers who share your desire to move forward. Seek out successful people and learn from their behavior. Surround yourself with people who are positive and supportive. All one has to do is watch the news or follow social media to see how much negativity there is in the world. It is easy to fall into the trap of becoming a victim and blaming others as the reason you're not succeeding. Avoid these people in both your personal and professional life.

I'll share a personal story to illustrate this point. Early in my career, I was asked to make a presentation in front of a large group. Several others in my peer group were also required to give a presentation at the same time. I spent a significant amount of time preparing and practicing, and when all the presentations were done, my project was chosen. I knew when I was done, I had hit a home run. When the dust settled, I expected that my peers who also made presentations would congratulate me for a job well done. Instead, I was castigated for making the rest of the group look bad. My response to them was that maybe they ought to step up their game and quit worrying about my work. I quickly distanced myself from these coworkers and sought people who shared the same passion to move forward that I had.

CHAPTER 14
Toot Your Own Horn

One of the techniques I used to ensure that I got credit for the work I did was to make sure the proper people were aware of my contributions. This can be tricky and requires professional decorum. Hanging banners off the company building declaring your prowess is not going to win you many friends. Here are a few of the techniques that have worked well for me over the years.

1. Ask for an audience in front of the company decision makers, which would include your boss, when presenting ideas that will increase revenue, decrease costs, or increase profitability.

2. Understand how your annual performance appraisal works and make sure you have properly documented your accomplishments throughout the twelve-month review period. For most managers, completing performance reviews is akin to pulling

teeth. This is especially true for inexperienced managers. If you understand this, you can help your boss manage the performance review process. In my experience, most reviews are written at the last minute with usually the last forty-five days of your performance forming the basis of the review. This is especially true for the soft skills set such as teamwork, adaptability, and other nonmeasurable skills. If you understand this, you can manipulate the review process to work to your advantage.

a. Find out the exact date of your review. Ignore the calendar date range; chances are, the actual review may need to be completed after the last day of the calendar year. Once you know the date of the review, be on your best behavior for forty-five days prior to the review.

b. If possible, cherry-pick an important project— one that has income ramifications and is guaranteed to produce results—to conclude around the time of your annual review.

c. Ask your boss if you can write a draft of your own review without any grading, just text. Keep in mind your boss might be responsible for ten other reviews and most likely will never remember all of your accomplishments. Maintain a detailed journal of your accomplishments and results. With your detailed journal, it should be easy to write a review that details all of your accomplishments, making it easier for the boss to complete your review with all of your accomplishments properly documented.

3. If there is an employee-of-the-month or an employee-of-the-year award, ask your boss if your project qualifies you for one of these awards. These are soft awards and don't cost the company anything. Because these awards are easily referenced, they should come in handy at raise time.

4. If you get a chance, especially at review time, set up next year's review by asking if completing an agreed-upon task would be a consideration for a raise or bonus. Most companies have a section in the review in which they discuss next year's goals. This is the perfect opportunity to get your next year's raise on the record.

Following the above four steps will set you up for receiving an excellent review, especially if you truly are a top-20-percent contributor.

CHAPTER 15
Owning Up to Your Errors

One of the earliest and most important lessons I learned was to own up to errors I committed, and then implement a permanent solution that did not allow the error to reoccur. Everyone commits errors; they are inevitable. It is how you deal with them that can determine the final outcome. Dealing with errors is the reason that all companies have a customer service component in their management structure. A well-run company will acknowledge the error, investigate it, and implement a permanent solution. Think about situations when an error occurred and the company had a policy that properly addressed your concern. When this has happened to me, I remember how they handled my concern; if it was corrected to my satisfaction, I became a loyal customer. In my personal and professional life, I have remained a loyal customer of UPS. They have never failed to properly address issues I have had with them. Errors occur; it is how you address them that counts.

At the individual employee level, the same principles apply. Early in my career, a presentation that I was giving to upper management contained an error that was caught by someone in the audience. It was a technicality that did not dramatically impact the result I was trying to convey. When the error was pointed out, I blamed the computer program, and at that point I lost my audience. After the meeting, my boss pulled me into his office and told me how I should have handled the discovery of the error. My boss asked me if the error was material and could it have been fixed on the spot. I responded that it was not material, but I would have needed to fix the spreadsheet at my computer. (This was back in the days before Microsoft products.) My boss told me I should have asked everyone to correct their copies, continued with the presentation, and then immediately after the presentation issue a corrected copy to everyone in the room. The one lesson I took from this mentoring session was how you address your mistakes ultimately determines success or failure in a business environment.

There are two other important elements to owning up to one's errors. You cannot keep making the same error. If you do, it tells employers that you cannot learn from your own mistakes. You need to find the cause of the error and permanently correct it. Companies have had their reputations ruined by failing to correct their errors. A recent example is the ignition problem of US car manufacturer General Motors. Imagine how different events would have been if the ignition problem had been corrected properly as soon as it was identified. Another example would be a payroll clerk improperly paying an employee due to a keypunch error on the hourly pay rate. What if the payroll clerk was made aware of the error, but neglected to correct it? The same error would occur over and over again, until the cause of the error was corrected.

The last component to owning up to errors is to self-edit your work before submitting it. If you catch the error before submitting your work, then it is not an error. It becomes part of your process to ensure that you are putting out work you are proud to call your own. Self-editing includes matching expected results against the results you obtain when you've completed the task. A simple example illustrates this point. If you go to the store and purchase an item that has a price tag of $10, and the clerk tells you that you owe $100, clearly an error has occurred. You detected the error because your expectations were not met. The price tag stated $10 and you expected to pay $10, not $100. You would question the validity of the transaction before agreeing to pay. Once you understand what to expect, especially with tasks you do daily, self-editing becomes much easier. As we discussed in Chapter "10", self-editing can also include having someone else review your work if you cannot locate the error. It helps having a fresh set of eyes look at something. Another form of self-editing if you have the time is to let the work sit overnight, and then review it the next day when you have a clear mind.

CHAPTER 16
Be on Time

One easy habit that needs to be developed early in a career is being on time. This includes all aspects of professional life. Any commitment you make should have a time component to it.

Let's start from the beginning of the day to the end of a day. If your starting time is eight o'clock, then you should show up at eight o'clock or earlier. The reasoning behind showing up earlier is that almost everyone commutes by roadway; traffic is always subject to ebbs and flows. Leave enough time to account for all but the most unavoidable of circumstances. You do not want to have the reputation of someone who is always late in the morning. If you're late enough times, that reputation will stick with you for as long as you are with the company. It also causes problems for your employer, who now has to explain your actions to other employees. Your employer starts getting questions like, "Why can Johnny be late and I can't?" This is especially problematic if different managers are involved. Manager A might be tough on tardiness, but Manager B might have looser standards. In this scenario, expect a visit to the Human Resources office and disciplinary action. If you can't avoid being late, contact your manager personally—and before your expected arrival time. Don't forget to estimate when you expect to be at work. This way, your manager knows your whereabouts and can explain your absence if someone inquires about it.

Be on time or early for meetings. If everyone else can make it on time, so can you. There is nothing more annoying to the rest of the group than someone walking in after a meeting has started. Everyone stops what they are doing, draining the room of energy. I'm sure almost everyone has the same thought when someone walks into a meeting late: "If I can be on time, why can't this person?" If you are always late, no one will take you seriously even if you have something important to share.

During the typical workday, there are other commitments not to be late for, such as an invitation to lunch by your coworkers. If you're late, don't be surprised when other invitations start to dry up. A typical workday contains commitments of all types, such as deadlines to meet, people to see, and places to be. All of these commitments have a time element that requires you to be punctual.

In Chapter "3", we discussed deadlines and negotiating deadlines. Some of these concepts were discussed in depth, but they are worth going over again.

1. When setting a deadline for yourself, be aggressive but realistic. If the deadline is too loose, you risk losing the assignment to someone else. If the deadline is too tight, you risk making errors or missing the deadline. The next step is to make your deadline. If something unexpected develops, negotiate a new deadline within plenty of time so your boss has the option of accepting it or diverting additional resources if the deadline can't be rescheduled. For argument's sake, should you submit your completed work if you still have several days left on your deadline? This will be one of the few times I don't advise being early. Meeting an agreed-upon deadline early most likely will not get your work looked at any sooner; it will probably be reviewed when it was originally due. If you are habitually early when meeting deadlines, this can give the impression you were sandbagging and opens you up to be second-guessed. As your supervisor, knowing you're always early with assignments, I would start expecting work several days early and would quickly hold you to the more aggressive deadlines. If you finish your task early, take the extra time to revisit the work and self-edit it for errors.

2. When a deadline is set for you, make sure you don't blindly agree to it thinking it is the right thing to do. You will not get in trouble with your employer if you thoughtfully review what is needed to accomplish the task and ask for more time. If you cannot be given more time, ask for more resources. What if you are working on a project and someone gives you additional work with the same deadline as your current project? You have two choices:

   a. You can say nothing and set yourself up for frustration, or worse, failure.

   b. Calmly point out the particulars about the current project you are working on and ask your boss to prioritize the two projects. You will be surprised by the reaction you will receive. Most likely, your boss did not recall the first project. The boss should ask when you can complete the newest project. If both are critical and need to be completed at the same time, your boss should ask what would be needed to get them both done on time and accurately. Your response should be direct and specific as to what resources you will need, and that would include people if necessary.

We are now at the end of the day and it is time to leave. You should leave at the time you are scheduled to leave or later. Never leave early unless a prior arrangement with your boss has been agreed to.

A pet peeve of mine that is a bit off topic, but somewhat related to being on time, is employees who are sick and have someone else call in for them. Unless you are incapacitated in a manner where you physically cannot call in sick, it is imperative that you touch base with your boss about your absence. As soon as you are aware that you will be absent, call in and leave a voice mail, text, or some other method of communication prior to your start time. This allows the boss to make other arrangements. I would recommend following up once the office is open and directly talking to your boss, who can then ask any questions he may have of you. Doing nothing is not an option; the worst thing that can happen is your boss doesn't see you at your designated start time and launches a full-scale manhunt. If your boss has to call you first, that bad feeling that you're avoiding communicating your absence will never go away.

CHAPTER 17
Life Lessons Learned from Difficult Situations

Personally and professionally, everyone encounters roadblocks, challenges, personal loss, and heartbreak. These are part of the human condition. How we choose to handle these ultimately helps shape our character and allows us to appreciate the joy and happiness life brings. I want to concentrate here on accepting the challenges difficult professional situations provide, and can ultimately lead you to a more rewarding professional life. I believe personal examples can be the best teacher.

In my life, several events have shaped how I landed in the here and now. In 2002, I received last rites due to a liver ailment. When I entered the hospital, I was given a window of thirty-six hours. If I survived past the thirty-six hours, I could expect a full recovery; otherwise, I would die. I was lucid enough to make myself several promises, including publishing this book and not putting off until tomorrow what I could do today.

Another example of lessons learned from a difficult situation happened to me in the late 1990s. I was working in a manufacturing plant in Brooklyn that was struggling to survive. Most of us knew that it was only a matter of time before the facility would be shut down. I made a professional decision to see the process through to the end instead of seeking employment elsewhere. I felt at the time that I would benefit in the long run by experiencing a facility shutdown due to lack of profits. The plant was extremely efficient; there was just not enough business to support all the overhead.

One day, I showed up for work and was told to meet some corporate big shots from California later that day in New Jersey. I and another employee drove to New Jersey, and along the way, we discussed what corporate would want with the both of us. We came to the conclusion that we weren't being fired because firing us in tandem at the same meeting seemed unprofessional. We concluded that we were going to be told that the plant would be closing at the end of the year. It was already June, so six months' notice seemed about right.

We arrived at the meeting early and were asked if we had any idea why we were summoned. We both said that given how poorly the plant was performing, we felt that corporate was going to announce it would shut down the plant at the end of the year. We were half-right. The plant was shutting down, but shutting down on Friday morning. We were hearing this on Thursday evening. We were chosen to make sure the shutdown occurred as planned.

The plan was for the machinery and equipment to be shut down at six o'clock Friday morning. From a shipment and receiving of goods standpoint, nothing was going to be allowed to enter or leave the facility until outside labor from the New Jersey facility arrived on site. At the shift change, which was at eight o'clock, armed guards would arrive to issue final paychecks and escort all the employees out of the facility. Equipment (trucks and forklifts) and personnel (maintenance, production, and warehouse) would arrive by ten o'clock, and, OH, YEAH, this 250,000-square-foot facility had to be completely empty by midnight Sunday. The reason for this was that the union would receive a court order to padlock the facility on Monday morning. The goal was to have them padlock an empty building. We managed to complete the task on time.

Another task we were both assigned was that we had to provide corporate a list of employees we wanted to take with us to the New Jersey facility. The Brooklyn facility was being closed and all the equipment and inventory was going to be integrated into the New Jersey plant as part of a facility consolidation. Out of three hundred employees, I recommended seven; the other manager who handled production took approximately forty employees. This ties in nicely with Jack and Suzy Welch's 20–70–10 rule. At the time I didn't know about this, but instinctively we practiced it in making our choices of personnel to keep. Over time, I began to realize that 20 percent of a company's employees are indispensable.

What could I have possibly learned from this most difficult of situations? I learned that I was capable of performing and meeting deadlines under extreme duress. I learned I was capable of rational decision making in a chaotic situation. I learned I was capable of making harsh decisions regarding employees' livelihoods (not sure how proud I am of this). I constantly refer to these experiences to this day, armed with the knowledge I can function at a high level under the most extreme of deadlines.

The lesson here is that failure such as the one I experienced can provide accelerated professional growth that a stable employment situation cannot. Nothing teaches like experience. If faced with a situation in which you know the challenges are going to be great, running away from it may not be the best opportunity to grow professionally. As someone who hires, I'm always intrigued by people who choose to be a part of the solution, especially if they can relay back to me the experience they acquired by seeing something through to the end, even if the outcome was not ideal.

The next example occurred on September 11, 2001, when I was working in New Jersey. Due to the Brooklyn plant consolidation, we had approximately fifty employees who lived in New York City. Because it was a three-shift operation, we had them split about evenly among the shifts. We got in that morning, and soon after, rumors started circulating that a plane had hit the World Trade Center. Back in 2001, news was not instantaneous and the Internet on the office computers was very limited (we still worked on the old IBM legacy production software). I remember thinking that a small, two-seat airplane struck one of the towers and went about my business. Our switchboard operator started receiving calls from concerned family members as to where their loved ones were. At this point, we decided to set up an old television in our conference room; we got the rabbit ears going and picked up a local news feed. It was then we realized that the United States was under attack.

We met in the conference room and laid out a course of action to take care of our New York employees. Prior to shutting down the facility, we needed to make sure we could take care of their concerns. Communications were not as sophisticated as they are today, which created a unique set of challenges for the management team. We needed to make sure that none of our New York employees in the New Jersey facility had any loved ones at the World Trade Center site. Because all traffic in and out of New York City was suspended, we had to book hotel rooms and rental cars and purchase personal items such as clothing and food. We were each assigned a specific task that needed to be executed in a timely and empathetic manner. Our New York employees were cut off from their families, and they were looking to us to provide answers and solutions. Additionally, we needed to communicate with the rest of the New York employees who were not at the plant in New Jersey to make sure they did not require anything and let them know when the facility would be reopening.

We set up a communication area in the front office and worked through each employee's concerns and needs. By the end of the day, everyone was placed in a hotel, necessities purchased, and all loved ones contacted and accounted for. Only one of our employees had a loved one in or near the World Trade Center site. His shift in one of the towers had ended before the planes struck the building, but the concern was he occasionally worked overtime. He was located safely at home. There was one major lesson for me that day: whether you realize it, there is a sacred bond between employee and employer. It is a lesson I will never forget. If someone works for me, I try my best never to break that trust; if for some reason I unknowingly do something that shakes that trust, I make amends to immediately regain it.

CHAPTER 18
Methodically Plan for Your Next Job

Over the years, I have countless times witnessed an employee quitting a job out of frustration. I'm talking about a good solid employee who decides the grass has to be greener on the other side. (Employees terminated for cause: this lesson will not help you.) I've seen employees quit because they were working long hours with no end in sight, or they didn't like their boss, or didn't get the raise they expected—you name it, I've witnessed it. As an employee, this is the worst thing you can do for your long-term earning potential. Typically, what occurs is the employee will get another job in a similar pay range. The worst-case scenario is the employee leaves for what amounts to be the identical job. An employee who leaves in an emotional state most likely neglected to properly negotiate pay and participation in the next raise cycle, further damaging any long-range earning power.

In Chapter "5", we discussed that hard work never killed anyone. If you have an end game and goal in mind about the salary you want and a time frame to get it, you can endure any number of hardships. Using the lessons discussed in this book, if you properly plan out your job search, you will most likely find the type of job that helps you meet your salary goals. Never leave a job under anyone's terms but your own. This would include timing, pay, benefits, or whatever else is important to you. Once you find the job you feel gives you the best opportunity to improve yourself, make an unemotional decision about what is best for you and your family. I promise that your old company will survive without you. You are under no moral obligation to stay out of some false sense of duty. You owe the company you are leaving an acceptable amount of notice and an honest day's work every time you walk through the door. For that, you are paid a wage, and most likely get to come in the next day and start the process all over again.

An important component of leaving a job is self-awareness. We all, to some degree, have a different view of ourselves than how the outside world perceives us. Think of the number of times you have wondered about what a random person is wearing and think, "What was that person thinking?" or "What was that person looking at in the mirror?" The answer is probably as simple as they see themselves in a different light than everyone else does. The problem manifests itself when there is a lack of self-awareness. When you cannot put yourself in other people's shoes and try and see yourself as others see you, poor decisions might follow. A little story helps illustrate this.

A couple from a distant city is thinking about relocating to a smaller, quieter town. As the couple reaches the towns limits, they stop at a gas station. While filling up, they strike up a conversation with the gas attendant about looking to relocate for a less hectic lifestyle, and ask what the people are like in this town. The attendant asks the couple what the people were like in the big city where they lived. They tell the attendant that the neighbors are rude, unfriendly, and it's difficult to meet new people. The attendant tells the couple that the people in this town are much the same way. The couple thanks him and says they will check the next town to see if the people there are friendlier.

About an hour later, another couple from the same big city pulls up to the same gas station and the same gas attendant greets them. The couple strikes up a conversation and tells the attendant they are thinking about relocating, and ask what the people are like in town. The attendant asks the couple what were the people like in the big city they were from. They gush that they had wonderful neighbors, people accepted new neighbors with open arms, and they were going to miss all the friends they were leaving be-hind. The attendant tells the couple that the people in town are much the same way, and they should have no prob-lems making new friends. The couple tells the attendant it sounds like they have found the perfect town.

Leaving and finding a new job is much the same as in the example just presented. If you have trouble at your old job and you leave expecting the grass to be greener, you will most likely encounter the same problems in your new job. The one thing that both jobs have in common is you. You cannot run away from the person staring back at you in the mirror. If you leave your old job for all the right reasons—better opportunity, better pay, or whatever you deem important—you will find that your chances for success at your new job are vastly superior to the person who leaves thinking a change in scenery will solve every problem.

CHAPTER 19
Interviewing from an Interviewer's Perspective

There are literally thousands of books and seminars covering how to interview. I'm not going to address interviews from the interviewee's perspective, but from my own experiences as someone who has done hundreds of interviews and hired over a hundred employees. I want to give my perspective of what I consider important and what I look for as an interviewer. I'm not going to offer a do-and-don't list—except for one don't: don't apologize for your previous work experience.

When showing up for an interview, be prepared to be hired on the spot. My stepfather was a welder, and when he would look for work he would pack all of his welding gear and take it with him. He would show up at the interview in his welding outfit, including his welding hood. I asked him why he did this because he looked terrible in his over-alls, gloves, and welding hood. His response was spot-on: "What if they need me that day? Then I'm ready to work and they don't have to bother interviewing anyone else for my job." If you show up to my interview not prepared to work that same day, I disqualify you as a candidate.

Show up for the interview early. I would recommend fifteen minutes in case there is any paperwork to fill out prior to the start of the interview, such as applications and personal history. As the interviewer, I set a time and I expect the interview to start promptly. My assumption is you are intuitive enough to realize there might be other commitments prior to seeing me. If you show up to my interview fifteen minutes early, you're on time and I will consider you as a candidate.

Make sure you bring all of your appropriate documentation and a pen. It is not my job to provide you with a pen. Don't assume I have your résumé or whatever documentation you need to get the job.

I would recommend that you do some research on the company I work for. It is not that hard to find information on companies. If I ask you what you know about my company, I expect a well-thought-out response.

In my interview with you, I would like to hear about your accomplishments. Have them well documented. Be specific; define the problems you solved and goals you accomplished in very detailed terms in alignment with the job you are seeking.

Answer my questions honestly and directly. Give me some credit for understanding that the business you're leaving might be different than mine. Even though the companies might make their revenue differently, prepare your answers on how you handled challenges you faced. I'm interested in the process you go through to solve a problem, not the types of problems you solved.

Never apologize for the type of work you have done or your experiences if you have come by them honestly. When I interview candidates, I believe it is up to me to find the best one for the job. I have never limited myself to interviewing candidates from the same industry as I'm in. In some cases, that can't be avoided, but what I have experienced is that being in the same industry as the job you are seeking is irrelevant. An example of a hire I made will illustrate this point.

About ten years ago, I needed to hire an individual to prepare orders for several hundred retail locations spread across the United States and Canada. The orders were prepared based on information captured remotely from locations manned by employees with little or no professional experience. The job required inventory and accounting knowledge and, most important, exceptional communication skills with the ability to provide excellent customer service. I decided that having the communication and customer service skills was more important than the inventory and accounting skills. The industry that this person worked in was irrelevant to my search. The company I was working for was in the personal care industry, selling in a mall environment. The individual I hired came from an onion farm out of their administrative and accounting area. When I asked him to go through his day, he confidently told me that he prepared orders and communicated them to the fieldworkers on a daily basis. When I asked him how he did this, he said that he would walk out into the fields and tell the workers what to do. He said that most of the workers spoke only Spanish, and although he was not fluent in Spanish, he was able to overcome this by using numbers and illustrations. I hired him on the spot; my logic for doing so was that I had located a person who had exceptional communication skills and understood who his customers were: the fieldworkers.

I always felt it was up to me as the interviewer to determine what was most important to me and get the best candidates, regardless of the industry they came from.

CHAPTER 20
The Art of Prioritizing Your Own Time

In Chapter "3", we discussed goal setting, including short-term, midrange, and long-term goals. An important component of goal setting is negotiating a deadline. To negotiate deadlines, you must know what resources you will need to meet your stated goal on time. Resources include labor and capital. Depending upon the goal, labor resources could mean just your time or people from inside or outside the organization. The use of capital may be as simple as a computer, or could include money, equipment, and buildings. The art of prioritizing your time is part of knowing what resources you will need to meet your goals. In a general sense, I'm using prioritizing your time as a metaphor for prioritizing all of the resources you will need to meet a goal. As you take on more challenging tasks, the principles you would use with your time work the same even if you are commanding hundreds of people and millions of dollars' worth of revenue and equipment to meet your stated goals.

To illustrate the art of prioritizing your time, let's use the example of preparing daily shipments to be picked up by UPS at four o'clock. Your company policy states that any order received before noon will ship the same day. Any order received after noon will ship the next day. As the shipping supervisor, your job is to ensure that this flow of goods occurs, no exceptions. For our example, I'll discuss some of the more common issues that might cause daily shipments to be missed, all the while keeping in mind company policy.

From the company's perspective, no revenue is generated unless orders are turned into shipments and shipments into cash. It's clear from this example that the shipping supervisor plays a very important role in revenue generation for the company. As a shipping supervisor, what types of challenges would cause shipping delays?

1. Employees calling in sick
2. Computer systems not responding
3. Unexpected corporate meetings involving all personnel
4. Your boss redirecting your efforts

This list of issues could be endless; so for our example, we will concentrate on the four above. If you prioritize your time and your team's resources, there is no reason not to complete the shipping within company guidelines even under duress.

When employees call in sick, as the shipping supervisor, you should be prepared for this by cross-training your staff to carry out the responsibilities of the sick employee. You may have to redirect an employee's time to the essential task of daily shipments and allow other less critical tasks to be delayed.

If the company's computers are down, the act of physically packing and shipping goods must still continue. This may mean going to a manual system and entering the paperwork when the computers are working again. If the computer systems do not come back online prior to the four o'clock deadline, making it impossible to print shipping labels and transmit pickup instructions, it may mean driving the shipments to a local UPS hub.

Our third example of unexpected challenges is a meeting scheduled for all employees that might lead to missed shipments. All companies with astute upper management understand that essential tasks need to be accomplished regardless of the circumstances. As the shipping supervisor, it is your job to prioritize what is needed to accomplish essential tasks and make sure the resources are committed. As a department manager, if one of my supervisors didn't speak up that they were in danger of missing a critical deadline, my assumption was that they had everything under control. I would never allow a supervisor to use me as the excuse for missing a crucial deadline. It is the job of a supervisor to make sure these deadlines are met. When a supervisor is aware that a critical deadline could be missed due to resources being redeployed, the dialogue between manager and supervisor might go something like this. As the supervisor, I would ask for permission to excuse the following employees from the mandatory meeting in order to meet shipment deadlines. I would let the manager know that I will meet with these employees later in the day, after all the shipments are picked up, and fill them in on the details of the meeting. No boss would find fault with this well-thought-out request.

For our fourth challenge of having your boss redirect your team's efforts away from meeting daily shipments, renegotiate a new deadline for the additional assignment. If both deadlines are critical, ask for more resources so that both deadlines are done accurately and on time. (Refer to Chapter 3, "Negotiating Deadlines and Goals.")

The lesson I want to convey is, once you understand what is critical to your company's success, it is up to you to prioritize resources to ensure that they get done accurately and on time.

CHAPTER 21
It's Never Over until It's Over

When I graduated from college in 1978, I was excited to receive what I considered was my first real job offer: an auditor for a bank in Pittsburgh. I was full of ideas and I was going to change the world as I steadily climbed up the corporate ladder. Soon after, reality set in, and within a year I left Pittsburgh for the greener pastures of Southern California, which was like moving to heaven for an inner-city young adult. In my first few years in California, I had three jobs, along with six months of self-imposed unemployment to enjoy the California lifestyle. I soon began to think I had wasted my first four years out of college.

But in hindsight, those four years prepared me for what was to come. I was smart, energetic, aggressive, and extremely unproductive, jumping from job to job with basically the same pay I received when I first graduated from college.

Looking back, I realized I was ready for something different, and I accepted a position with a company that manufactured plastic containers. It was at this company that I reached out to a mentor to ask how to earn more money. As I discussed previously, my mentor had me work as a supervisor on the weekend night shifts along with my regular staff accounting job during the week to prepare me for additional job responsibilities. While I had an audience with my mentor, I asked another important question that serves as an example of it's never over until it's over. I asked him why no one took my ideas seriously. I knew my ideas were good, yet when I brought them up, they never seemed to get put into motion.

As an employee, nothing is more demotivating than having good ideas that are not taken seriously. When looking back, I see this led me to job hop for four years because I felt that no one was taking me seriously and the next job had to be better. My mentor helped me to understand that getting your ideas put into motion is a process. (For presenting an idea or concept, go back to Chapter 9, "Thinking for Your Boss.") You can't just present an idea, concept, or problem without specifics. That is nothing more than noise in your boss's day.

Understanding that your boss is facing all the same challenges you do on a daily basis will help you get your ideas and concepts put into place. Have empathy for your boss, walk a mile in his shoes. Your boss may hear your idea and agree with you that yes, something should happen, and then reality sets in and your idea stagnates. You get frustrated and feel no one appreciates all the hard work you do. Another way to look at your idea stagnating is, it might be as simple as your boss is busy and lost track of your idea. Find the right opportunity and bring it up again. The right time could be during the annual review process, when you have the ideal opportunity to set goals for the coming year. If your idea involves spending money, understanding your company's finances might offer insight as to when to present your idea again. Most companies do their budgets for the upcoming year late in the previous year; an understanding of this process might get your idea in front of the budget committee for consideration. Generating a new idea early in a new year may just mean that all resources have already been committed, and you will need to resubmit at the appropriate time for the next budget cycle. Another excellent time to present ideas is when there is a change in management. For example, if your boss quits and was sitting on several of your ideas, submit them to your new boss and have a fresh pair of eyes look at them.

The answer to the question I asked my mentor years ago of why no one took my ideas seriously is simple: "Just because I'm not jumping out of my chair over your idea does not mean it is not a good one; it only means I'm busy. It's your job to keep reminding me, and until I say no or throw you out of my office, I expect you to keep reminding me".

CHAPTER 22
Seek Perfection in Small Bites

Seeking perfection can seem like a daunting challenge that cannot be attained. Understanding what you are chasing and how it can be attained will quickly separate you from the pack, and earn you a reputation as a top performer. Being able to put a plan in place to pursue perfection is what all companies strive for—and will pay good salaries for. To illustrate my point, let's use an example all of us are familiar with: striving to reach our ideal body weight. If you pick up any diet book, any how-to video, or any exercise book, the principles are all the same. The methods used to reach the goal most certainly will be different because there are many ways to reach one's ideal body weight.

Staying with our body weight theme, a long-range goal for John is 200 pounds. To determine how best to arrive at that goal, John needs to assess how much he currently weighs. He steps on a scale and records a weight of 250 pounds. John can now devise a road map to meet his perfect weight of 200 pounds.

The second step is to pick the deadline date at which he will attain his perfect weight of 200 pounds. John sits down and decides that if he follows his plan, in six months he should be able to reach his goal. This all sounds well and good except for one detail: reaching the goal is daunting, and without proper measurement and feedback statistics, John's quest is doomed to failure.

Statistically, John has an 80 percent chance of failure, or a 20 percent chance of success. The success rate of 20 percent coincides nicely with the lessons we have discussed in previous chapters. To achieve success in business, you need to be considered a top performer, and typically that is reserved for the top 20 percent of employees. With these success rate figures in mind, how can John significantly increase his chances of meeting his ideal body weight?

I have found that having three to five ideal body weight goals in support of the final goal significantly increases the rate of success. If John has only one goal, he will have only one chance to celebrate his success, which is at the end of a very long and arduous process. However, if he has a number of smaller goals, he gets multiple times to celebrate. Another crucial step in achieving his overall goal is that John gets feedback that what he is doing is working and, possibly even more important, what is not working. This feedback is valuable because it allows John to course correct if necessary, or if he is making steady progress, to continue to do what he outlined.

John lays out a plan to lose ten pounds in the first two weeks, and five pounds the next two weeks, and then seven pounds a month after that, which will allow him to reach his goal of losing fifty pounds in six months. It's one thing to put numbers on paper, but John has to make significant changes to his current way of operating to achieve these goals. To support his overall goal, John commits to three specific tasks: he will invest in a gym membership, he will consult weekly with diet and exercise experts, and he will measure and record his weight on a weekly basis. By following these three steps, John will be able to determine if additional investment in time and money will be needed to achieve his goal. John is now ready to embark on his plan of achieving his perfect body weight.

John stays on course with the tasks he outlined for his diet and exercise plan. After one month, John weighs 234 pounds, putting him slightly ahead of the one-month goal of 235 pounds. He now has the opportunity to step back and celebrate meeting his goal. Just because John meets his first goal does not mean his journey is over. He now starts the process all over again as he has a new goal of losing seven pounds so that he weighs 228 pounds at the end of the second month.

Not every step will be smooth in your pursuit of perfection, and in our example, neither is John's. After two weeks into the second month, John's weight is still 234 pounds. He has been following his plan, but with no results. He now must review what he is doing and decide whether to continue with his plan or modify it. After meeting with his diet and exercise team, John decides to modify what he has been doing. He makes the following minor corrections: his exercise plan was developed for a beginner, so the decision was made to increase the intensity. After reviewing John's diet journal, it was determined that his diet did not require any changes, and that increasing the intensity of the exercise should get him back on track. John steps on the scale after week three and he now weighs 230 pounds; at the end of the second month, he meets his goal of 228 pounds. John celebrates reaching his interim goal and continues with his quest for the perfect body weight.

I could have inserted almost any goal or situation where striving for perfection is the ultimate goal. If you seek perfection in small bites and make use of measurement and feedback to guide you, progress toward perfection is possible.

CHAPTER 23
Random Thoughts

In writing this book I had a collection of ideas that did not warrant being treated as a lesson, but I felt they were important enough to mention to spur thought.

Pay attention to your overall physical fitness. This may not be politically correct, but over the years, I have noticed that people in good physical condition were more apt to receive choice assignments and monetary awards than employees who were not fit. The theme of this book is to differentiate yourself so you can maximize your earning power, and maintaining your fitness can be a factor. Please note I did not use the words *physically attractive*, but *physical fitness*, which can be controlled by most of us. The rigors of early adulthood are great, and I believe a certain level of fitness and stamina needs to be maintained to properly manage all the demands placed on young adults. Typically, young professionals are working full time, going to school, starting families, setting up households, and in some cases, all of the above. To accomplish these and stay productive requires a certain level of fitness.

If you watch the news on a daily basis, you will hear that jobs are being taken away from hardworking people and given to people who don't deserve them. This argument is best left to politicians and special interest groups. For the rest of us, I have news for you: it is not your job if someone else occupies it. I want to focus on what this statement means to you. You cannot worry about a job that someone else occupies. You are only hurting yourself if you think you're being held back because the job someone else is doing really belongs to you. If you're reading this book, some of the lessons discussed can help you get the job that starts you on the path to the middle class.

In the same vein, stop comparing your pay to what other people earn as this has nothing to do with what you earn. Early in my career, I was responsible for payroll in a large manufacturing plant. I took a hard look at what people were making and compared that to what I made. All range of emotions popped up: anger, envy, and depression, to name a few. I felt I was more important to the company in terms of revenue than some of the employees who were earning more than I was. I felt I was a superior worker to many of my high-earning coworkers. It was depressing and demotivating. Luckily, I had a mentor who was not involved with this company who was able to quickly help me sort out my feelings. It was around this time that my understanding of compensation and the Rule of 72 took root. The first lesson I received is that I was a poor negotiator, and the people earning the higher salaries did a better job of negotiating their compensation. This book is proof I took that advice to heart.

The second lesson learned was that all companies have a salary structure, and they value the job, not the person. If that job becomes vacant for any reason, the next person occupying that job will make the same salary.

The third lesson was, if you're not happy with your compensation, do something about it; complaining about it or letting it rule your emotions won't put more money in your pocket.

Avoid this trap at all costs as you embark on your career journey: what other people earn has absolutely nothing to do with what you should be trying to accomplish.

Late in my career, I heard the saying "Sit in the outer tent," and was pleased to know that there was a behavior to describe what everyone eventually will need to do to get an important task completed. Everyone has come across a situation that in order to finish a task, you will need the direct help of someone who holds a key piece required for completion. An example would be a smog inspection needed for you to complete your yearly car registration. To register your car, you need a smog test and a certificate to send in with your payment. I have had instances where the smog attendant was at lunch and I have parked my car in the spot where the test would occur and waited until he returned from lunch. I was not leaving without my certificate. The smog station was the inner tent, and I parked my car where he could see it: in the outer tent.

A professional example would be when there is an absolute critical deadline whose completion solely relies on the signature of a specific individual. I had this occur recently where a signature was required to get a shipment released from impound. It was a shipment of components required to complete a multimillion-dollar order. If the order wasn't released by a specific date, millions of dollars' worth of product with a shelf life would spoil. The person I was looking for was in a meeting behind closed doors, and the secretary wouldn't let me interrupt. At that point, I had two choices: wait and risk missing the shipment, or interrupt the meeting and get the signature. I chose to interrupt the meeting, and for my efforts received both a lecture and praise the next day. The closed-door meeting represented the inner tent, and I was positioned outside of the office, or in the outer tent; leaving without the signature was not an option.

The lesson of the outer tent is that you have to own your own work and ideas. The way I'm able to internalize this and decide what my responsibilities are is to envision what the final outcome is. An example I use is, if you produce the finest widget in the world and you sell it in the most exclusive shops, the job is still not complete. The job is complete when you collect the money from the customer and safely deposit it in the bank. Until all these steps are properly completed, there may come a time when you need to sit in the outer tent.

One of the mistakes that both companies and individuals make is to overvalue individuals who put out fires. (I don't mean this in the literal sense of our emergency personnel who fight fires and save lives.) I'm talking about the individual who waits until problems deteriorate to the point where you have to gut the operation and start over again. From observing this behavior over the years, what strikes me is that this type of employee seems to get an adrenaline rush out of going into an out-of-control situation and getting it back on its feet. I also noticed that some companies reward this type of management style and encourage this behavior. At the other end of the spectrum are employees who quietly create value and run a steady ship, but are ignored. As the saying goes, the squeaky wheel gets the grease. I gave a name to those individuals who rush in to fix out-of-control problems: firefighters. I believe that a majority of these firefighters actually set the fires that they have to put out, and to make matters worse, were rewarded for it.

There are several common traits shared by the firefighter.

1. Procrastination—The firefighter kicks the issue causing the problem down the road until it explodes and can't be ignored.

2. Afraid of conflict resolution—An excellent example of this is when two employees have a problem with each other and their firefighter supervisor turns a blind eye, hoping it will resolve itself. Once it erupts into a full-blown crisis, the firefighter has to take action, most likely at a great cost of jobs and reputations. If the firefighter had confronted the problem early on and resolved it before it erupted, both employees probably would have come away with their jobs and reputations intact with nothing more than a slap on the wrist.

3. Neglect of routine tasks—The firefighter enjoys the exciting parts of the job and ignores the routine, such as balancing a cash drawer, counting inventory, or taking out the trash. With no one insisting that these routine tasks be completed, eventually someone from the outside locates theft, finds there is inventory missing, or shuts down a restaurant for a health violation. At this point, the firefighter rushes in and fires employees, or cleans up the restaurant for the follow-up inspection.

There are many more examples, but they all share the themes of procrastination, neglect, and lack of follow-up or follow-through, which eventually leads to a full-blown crisis in which the firefighter gets to shine. If you look deeper, more often than not the same person who caused the fire is the person who puts out the fire.

Made in the USA
Las Vegas, NV
09 December 2020